EU GDPR

An international guide to compliance

EU GDPR

An international guide to compliance

ALAN CALDER

IT Governance Publishing

IT Governance Publishing Ltd
Unit 3, Clive Court
Bartholomew's Walk
Cambridgeshire Business Park
Ely, Cambridgeshire
CB7 4EA
United Kingdom
www.itgovernancepublishing.co.uk

Formerly published as _EU GDPR – A pocket guide, second edition_ by IT Governance Publishing.

EU GDPR – An international guide to compliance first published in the United Kingdom in 2020 by IT Governance Publishing.

ISBN 978-1-78778-252-5

ABOUT THE AUTHOR

Alan Calder is the CEO of GRC International Group plc, the AIM-listed company that owns IT Governance Ltd (*www.itgovernance.co.uk*), an information, advice and consultancy firm that helps company boards tackle IT governance, risk management, compliance and information security issues. Alan is an acknowledged international cyber security guru and a leading author on information security and IT governance issues. He has many years of senior management experience in the private and public sectors.

CONTENTS

INTRODUCTION

Few companies are in favour of further regulation, but it is generally recognised that it has a role to play in keeping industries honest and protecting the populace at large. There is also a lot of opposition to particularly strong regulation, so more heavy-handed laws are often developed incrementally, which conveniently reduces the outcry at any given stage. It's quite rare for a particularly strong regulation to come about all at once: the European Union's General Data Protection Regulation (GDPR) is one such beast, however.

It's not that the GDPR is unnecessary, nor that any individual requirement is particularly egregious; rather, much of the initial challenge arose because it came along all at once and potentially affected nearly every organisation in the world. The Regulation is so widely applicable, in fact, that there are likely to be legal arguments and discussions over the coming decade to determine the true extent of its powers[1]. Since then, the challenge for many organisations has been to maintain compliance in the face of changing economies and the results of various legal cases, which have had some fundamental impacts on how the Regulation should be interpreted and applied.

The repercussions of failing to comply with the law are not to be sneezed at: organisations found to be in breach of the Regulation can be fined up to €20 million, or four percent of global annual turnover – whichever is greater. Needless to say, there are few

---

[1] There's more on this in chapter 3 of this guide (The Regulation).

companies that would be willing to take a hit of that magnitude when compliance can be achieved much more cheaply.

Equally, however, the Regulation aims to tread that line between protecting the rights of the individual and removing barriers to the "free movement of personal data within the internal market". That is, although the Regulation places limits and restrictions on the use and storage of personal data (sometimes called 'personally identifiable information', or PII), it does so in the interests of both keeping the EU at the forefront of the modern information economy while creating a 'level playing field' among EU Member States.

The organisations that appreciate this distinction – and act quickly to resolve issues and to ensure compliance with the Regulation – are those that thrive in an evolving regulatory environment.

This pocket guide aims to help your organisation thrive under the GDPR wherever you are in the world by providing you with an understanding of the Regulation, the broader principles of data protection, and what the Regulation means for businesses in Europe and beyond.

There are key terms throughout this book that need to be properly understood to really get to grips with the Regulation. These are defined in chapter 2 – Terms and definitions.

CHAPTER 1: A BRIEF HISTORY OF DATA PROTECTION

The common conception of data protection is a very modern notion. We think of digitally stored databases and records, and we understand the importance of protecting them. It's obvious: digital records have no physical weight and can be mislaid or stolen without removing the original, and it's easy to comprehend that such a loss could represent an enormous amount of information. This isn't the way it's always been, though, and even today information in other formats needs to be protected.

Possibly the earliest forms of data and privacy protection come from the professions rather than legislation itself. For instance, lawyer-client confidentiality (or legal professional privilege, as it's called in the UK) is believed to have begun as a sort of contract between a lawyer and their client many decades (and possibly centuries) before it entered into law itself. It was introduced as a way of ensuring that a lawyer could adequately represent their clients' interests without the client fearing legal repercussions.

Equally, the keeping of medical records and a doctor's confidentiality were established decades ago, and, although a court could force those records to be handed over, the medical profession was otherwise expected to keep them relatively safe. Once again, this was something that the profession handled long before the law moved to codify the practice.

Under these practices, specific silos of personal information were protected according to the interests of the business: if a profession could see the business value in protecting information, it was protected. This has had to change, however, as record keeping shifted from paper to electronics and as the methods for manipulating even small elements of personal information have become more powerful, which puts all this information at risk because it now has a distinct value. Political campaigns, as a *reasonably* ethical example, have used increasing volumes of data to better target key demographics, define policy, manage candidates' image and so on. On the other end of the scale, identity theft has become a significant problem that has only become a greater threat with the greater volume of information that is available.

With regard to the situation in Europe, one of the first legal protections for personal information was codified in Article 8 of the European Convention on Human Rights (ECHR) in 1953. This wasn't in the form that we might expect to see privacy legislation today, but it provides the foundation for modern European privacy laws. Article 8 reads:

1. Everyone has the right to respect for his private and family life, his home and his correspondence.

2. There shall be no interference by a public authority with the exercise of this right except such as is in accordance with the law and is necessary in a democratic society in the interests of national security, public safety or the economic well-being of the country, for the prevention of disorder or crime, for the protection of health or morals, or for the protection of the rights and freedoms of others.

There is some criticism that this is an unnecessarily open-ended provision, as unscrupulous people could interpret it in order to restrict the rights of the people (through the application of laws to circumvent some of the protections, which are permitted), to place undue regulatory burden on third parties (through the application of laws that use equally broad language) and to limit the power of the state to pursue justice (because the European Court of Human Rights will almost always find against any laws that could violate the right to privacy).[2] Obviously, these are conflicting opinions, so it has remained generally balanced in the interests of all parties.

Regardless of its interpretation, the ECHR's legacy with regard to the right to privacy has carried down through the decades into our modern legal landscape.

In 1981, the Council of Europe established standards to ensure the free flow of information throughout EU Member States without infringing personal privacy. The convention that enacted these standards – the Convention for the Protection of Individuals with regard to Automatic Processing of Personal Data – was developed in response to the burgeoning use of computers to store and process personal data. The minimum standards it set then became the basis of the first round of privacy laws across Europe.

In 1984, the UK introduced its first Data Protection Act, which introduced basic rules governing the storage and processing of personal data in the UK. These rules accommodated the minimum standards specified in the EU's 1981 convention, and thus weren't particularly rigorous – in 1984, of course, requirements for the protection of personal data were considerably less urgent than today.

As we know, however, the power and availability of computers exploded during the 80s and 90s, and by 1995 more than a million people in the UK were regularly using the Internet. Furthermore, over the years since the Convention was applied, EU Member States' data protection laws had diverged, which

---

[2] Especially if those laws seem to contravene or impinge on other articles in the ECHR, such as Article 10 – the right to freedom of expression and information.

began impeding the flow of data through the European Union – and thus impeding business. It was quite clear that existing data protection regimes across Europe were inadequate to support Articles 8 and 10 of the ECHR, and so the Data Protection Directive (DPD) was enacted in 1995.

The DPD required EU Member States to respond by developing laws of their own to meet new, more rigorous minimum standards, and taking into account the significantly more powerful, readily available and affordable computers and electronic devices. It was functionally a 'reset' for data protection, obliging all Member States to align with it and thereby improve protections for personal data, while simultaneously reducing the burdens impeding the free flow of data through the Union.

The DPD also established rules for the transport of personal data outside of the EU. This was most famously reflected in the US-EU Safe Harbor framework, which asserted that US data protection laws were sufficient for the protection of personal data originating in the EU, as long as the recipient in the US observed a set of data protection principles. While this framework was found to be in breach of the DPD in 2015, it did support considerable business activity for 15 years.

The UK's Data Protection Act of 1998 was the British law that enacted the requirements of the DPD and was founded on eight principles. These principles clearly laid out the general aims of the Act, which made it reasonably simple to determine whether an organisation was meeting its obligations. There was some complexity in the broader Act, however, and repeated amendments and updates meant that it continued to grow and become more unwieldy as time went on.

In Germany, meanwhile, data protection was primarily regulated through the Federal Data Protection Act (Bundesdatenschutzgesetz, BDSG), supported by a number of sector-specific regulations at varying levels of federal and state government. Because it also sought to meet the requirements of the DPD, this law was broadly comparable to the UK's DPA, but with considerable differences in the detail.

France's Data Protection Act (Loi informatique et libertés, LIL) dates back to 1978, predating many other national data protection laws and covering the lifespan of both the EU convention and the DPD. Rather than developing new laws in response to those pressures from the European Union, the French legislature instead opted to amend its existing law. Despite this, the LIL we see today is surprisingly concise.

Across the EU, similar legislation was enacted, but through a combination of time and varying national interests, no two national laws were sufficiently similar for an organisation to simultaneously be compliant in its home country and across all the other EU Member States. That is, the free flow of information was effectively inhibited because the different regulatory environments clashed on matters of detail, requiring businesses and governments alike to arrange processes specific to an increasing array of scenarios. It is this, in conjunction with the steady march of technological progress, that created the environment into which the General Data Protection Regulation was born.

That the solution is a regulation rather than a directive (as the DPD was) is worthy of discussion. Within EU law, a directive sets out minimum conditions or requirements but does not pass any specific measures in itself. That is, an individual or organisation is not required to be in compliance with a directive. Rather, each Member State is obliged to pass its own laws in order to meet the minimum requirements of the directive, and this is what organisations and individuals have to comply with.

A regulation, meanwhile, is functionally a law and enters into force across the Union simultaneously. No Member State needs to pass additional laws in order to bring it into force, and it is not dependent on the interpretation of the local government, courts or authorities. Because of the legal weight of a regulation, they typically take much longer to pass through the legislative process, but they also ensure greater consistency across the Union.

The GDPR had a particularly long and arduous journey on its way to approval by the European Parliament and Council, and it was not without controversy. However, over the several years it spent in committee stages, being written and rewritten – it had thousands of amendments proposed, pushing for more or less data privacy – the more contentious points were gradually eradicated.

The UK government chose to implement the GDPR via the UK Data Protection Act 2018, which received royal assent on 25 May 2018. The Act has transposed the GDPR into UK law. This means that, despite leaving the EU, companies in the UK will still be required to meet requirements equivalent to those of the GDPR.

While the GDPR is not law in other countries outside the EU, it is effectively part of the legislative environment for organisations that do business with the EU. This is enforced through a combination of international trade law and business pressure – after all, a partner in the EU is unlikely to want to risk engaging with a company in the US, Australia or Singapore (or anywhere else) that will put them at risk.

CHAPTER 2: TERMS AND DEFINITIONS

Before getting into the meat of the Regulation and how you can comply with it, it's useful to have a set of definitions for common and useful terms. Where the Regulation provides a definition, this is included, and any additional commentary has been added where useful. Terms are presented in alphabetical order.

Binding corporate rules

> personal data protection policies which are adhered to by a controller or processor established on the territory of a Member State for transfers or a set of transfers of personal data to a controller or processor in one or more third countries within a group of undertakings, or group of enterprises engaged in a joint economic activity;[3]

Binding corporate rules were originally devised by the Article 29 Working Party (a group within the EU that develops and promotes good practices for data protection and is now known as the European Data Protection Board) in order to allow large organisations, or groups of organisations, to securely transfer data internationally while reducing bureaucratic interference. The GDPR establishes conditions for individual Member States to establish their own binding corporate rules to streamline international transfers. At the end of the UK's transition period, the Information Commissioner's Office (ICO) will no longer be able to approve any binding corporate rules, so any such existing

---

[3] EU GDPR, Article 4 (20).

arrangements will need to be reapproved by a supervisory authority within one of the remaining Member States.

Biometric data

> personal data resulting from specific technical processing relating to the physical, physiological or behavioural characteristics of a natural person, which allow or confirm the unique identification of that natural person, such as facial images or dactyloscopic data;[4]

Biometric data is increasingly used as a method of authentication, and often in conjunction with other data that should be protected (such as passwords, and, by extension, whatever information can be accessed as a result of gaining access to this). Member States are permitted to introduce further restrictions or conditions regarding the processing of biometric data.

Consent

> any freely given, specific, informed and unambiguous indication of the data subject's wishes by which he or she, by a statement or by a clear affirmative action, signifies agreement to the processing of personal data relating to him or her;[5]

Consent is an important concept in the GDPR and is covered extensively later in this book.

---

[4] EU GDPR, Article 4 (14).

[5] EU GDPR, Article 4 (11).

Cross-border processing

a) processing of personal data which takes place in the context of the activities of establishments in more than one Member State of a controller or processor in the Union where the controller or processor is established in more than one Member State; or

b) processing of personal data which takes place in the context of the activities of a single establishment of a controller or processor in the Union but which substantially affects or is likely to substantially affect data subjects in more than one Member State.[6]

This refers to data transfers within the European Union; where this occurs, the Regulation has stipulations as to which supervisory authority is to be involved.

Data concerning health

personal data related to the physical or mental health of a natural person, including the provision of health care services, which reveal information about his or her health status;[7]

Health data is awarded particular protections under the Regulation in order to protect the vulnerable. While all personal data must be protected, some forms – such as health data – have additional restrictions as to how and when it can be processed, and the level of consent required to authorise the processing.

---

[6] EU GDPR, Article 4 (23).

[7] EU GDPR, Article 4 (15).

Member States are permitted to introduce further restrictions or conditions regarding the processing of data concerning health.

Data controllers

> the natural or legal person, public authority, agency or other body which, alone or jointly with others, determines the purposes and means of the processing of personal data; where the purposes and means of such processing are determined by Union or Member State law, the controller or the specific criteria for its nomination may be provided for by Union or Member State law;[8]

The key factor identifying the data controller is that they determine the "purposes and means" of processing personal data. These are usually the 'public-facing' entities that data subjects supply their information to. For instance, a hospital might have an online form for entering health information; even if the online form is provided by a third party, the hospital (which will determine what the data is processed for) will be the data controller. A data controller might do all of its processing in-house, or it might outsource some processing to data processors.

Data processors

> a natural or legal person, public authority, agency or other body which processes personal data on behalf of the controller;[9]

It is important to note that an organisation can be a data controller for one processing activity and a data processor for

---

[8] EU GDPR, Article 4 (7).

[9] EU GDPR, Article 4 (8).

another. In the example above, the organisation that provides the online form will be a data processor because the act of collecting data is included within the definition of 'processing', but it will be the data controller for processing activities relating to its own HR.[10] A single data controller may have several data processors.

Data subject

The Regulation defines a data subject as "an identified or identifiable natural person".[11] There is no restriction on their nationality or place of residence, so a data subject can be from anywhere in the world – the Regulation does not distinguish. However, a data subject has to be a *person*; a corporation or other entity cannot be a data subject, and information on those subjects has no protection under the Regulation.

Filing system

> any structured set of personal data which are accessible according to specific criteria, whether centralised, decentralised or dispersed on a functional or geographical basis;[12]

This is used as a generic term to cover all methods by which personal data can be collected, stored, transmitted and processed.

Genetic data

> personal data relating to the inherited or acquired genetic characteristics of a natural person which give unique

---

[10] EU GDPR, Article 4 (2).

[11] EU GDPR, Article 4 (1).

[12] EU GDPR, Article 4 (6).

information about the physiology or the health of that natural person and which result, in particular, from an analysis of a biological sample from the natural person in question;[13]

With the increasing interest in genetics and genetic engineering, and public concerns over the legal status of genetic data, the Regulation includes genetic data as part of personal data, thereby providing it with protections at least equal to other personal data. Member States are permitted to introduce further restrictions or conditions regarding the processing of genetic data.

Main establishment

a) as regards a controller with establishments in more than one Member State, the place of its central administration in the Union, unless the decisions on the purposes and means of the processing of personal data are taken in another establishment of the controller in the Union and the latter establishment has the power to have such decisions implemented, in which case the establishment having taken such decisions is to be considered to be the main establishment;

b) as regards a processor with establishments in more than one Member State, the place of its central administration in the Union, or, if the processor has no central administration in the Union, the establishment of the processor in the Union where the main processing activities in the context of the activities of an establishment of the processor take place to the extent that

---

[13] EU GDPR, Article 4 (13).

the processor is subject to specific obligations under this Regulation;[14]

Determining the 'main establishment' for organisations with a presence in multiple Member States is important, as this defines which supervisory authority is to be involved, and may have some impact on various restrictions and conditions on processing certain types of personal data (such as biometric, genetic and health data).

Personal data

> 'personal data' means any information relating to an identified or identifiable natural person ('data subject'); an identifiable natural person is one who can be identified, directly or indirectly, in particular by reference to an identifier such as a name, an identification number, location data, an online identifier or to one or more factors specific to the physical, physiological, genetic, mental, economic, cultural or social identity of that natural person;[15]

Of specific note here is that the set of characteristics above is not exhaustive: *any* information that could be used to identify the data subject is personal data, and this information can be in any format. This can encompass photographs, correspondence, physical media and so on. In 2016, the Court of Justice of the European Union ruled that IP addresses can also be considered personal data in circumstances where there is sufficient information to link the IP address to an individual.

---

[14] EU GDPR, Article 4 (16).

[15] EU GDPR, Article 4 (1).

Personal data breach

> a breach of security leading to the accidental or unlawful destruction, loss, alteration, unauthorised disclosure of, or access to, personal data transmitted, stored or otherwise processed;[16]

The majority of data breaches that the Regulation is concerned with are personal data breaches. More general data breaches will be of concern if the data that is lost could lead to a personal data breach.

Processing

> 'processing' means any operation or set of operations which is performed on personal data or on sets of personal data, whether or not by automated means, such as collection, recording, organisation, structuring, storage, adaptation or alteration, retrieval, consultation, use, disclosure by transmission, dissemination or otherwise making available, alignment or combination, restriction, erasure or destruction;[17]

This is an extremely broad definition but, again, is not exhaustive. Functionally, processing may include any interaction you have with personal data, in whatever form it takes. Note in particular that this includes storing information, even if you do nothing else with it. Establishing the full range of processing that you are responsible for is a significant part of complying with the Regulation.

---

[16] EU GDPR, Article 4 (12).

[17] EU GDPR, Article 4 (2).

Profiling

> any form of automated processing of personal data consisting of the use of personal data to evaluate certain personal aspects relating to a natural person, in particular to analyse or predict aspects concerning that natural person's performance at work, economic situation, health, personal preferences, interests, reliability, behaviour, location or movements;[18]

Data subjects must always be informed if any profiling processes will be performed on their personal data before they consent.

Pseudonymisation

> the processing of personal data in such a manner that the personal data can no longer be attributed to a specific data subject without the use of additional information, provided that such additional information is kept separately and is subject to technical and organisational measures to ensure that the personal data are not attributed to an identified or identifiable natural person;[19]

While the Regulation generally considers pseudonymisation to be a positive thing, it does also specify that pseudonymised data that can be "attributed to a natural person by the use of additional information should be considered to be information on an identifiable natural person".[20] As such, any organisation that uses pseudonymisation to protect personal data should ensure that it is not possible to identify the original data subject if

---

[18] EU GDPR, Article 4 (4).

[19] EU GDPR, Article 4 (5).

[20] EU GDPR, Recital 26.

additional information is made available. As noted in the definition, this should include measures to completely separate pseudonymised data from all other personal data.

Representative

> a natural or legal person established in the Union who, designated by the controller or processor in writing pursuant to Article 27, represents the controller or processor with regard to their respective obligations under this Regulation;[21]

Organisations (both data controllers and data processors) that are not established in the EU but wish to conduct processing in line with Article 27, must appoint a representative that is established in the EU. This ensures that all significant personal data collection and processing has a presence within the Union and ready contact with authorities.

At the time of writing, the European Commission has declared that the UK will become a "third country" under the GDPR at the end of the transition period (31 December 2020). Although the UK government is hoping a legally binding agreement between the UK and EU can be put in place, organisations in the UK will need to appoint a representative in the EU by the end of the transition period. It should also be noted that organisations wishing to process the personal data of UK residents after this date may need to establish a representative in the UK.

---

[21] EU GDPR, Article 4 (17)

Supervisory authority

> 'supervisory authority' means an independent public authority which is established by a Member State pursuant to Article 51;[22]

In most cases, the supervisory authority is the authority that was responsible for data protection measures prior to the GDPR. In Ireland, for instance, it is the Data Protection Commission.

---

[22] EU GDPR, Article 4 (21).

CHAPTER 3: THE REGULATION

The GDPR was adopted by the EU Council and Parliament in April 2016, and took effect in every EU Member State in May 2018. The GDPR is a long document, setting out requirements for organisations and for Member States, and making provision for an EU Data Protection Board. This chapter aims to provide a quick overview of the key points you need to be aware of to comply.

The full text of the GDPR can be found on the EUR-Lex database (*https://eur-lex.europa.eu/*) in every language of the European Union.[23]

Organisations based outside the EU should also look for guidance on complying with the GDPR from the supervisory authority in the Member State where they do the majority of their business or where the largest number of data subjects reside. For instance, if the majority of EU residents whose personal data you process are based in Greece, you should seek guidance from the Hellenic Data Protection Authority.

While you undoubtedly need to engage with your professional advisers to ensure that your legal documentation complies with the GDPR, this pocket guide gives you a far less expensive overview of the requirements.

Failure to meet the requirements could be costly. The Regulation specifies that administrative fines are to follow "appropriate

---

[23] The full text of the Regulation can be found in English at *http://eur-lex.europa.eu/legal-content/EN/TXT/PDF/?uri=CELEX:52012PC0011&rid=2*.

procedural safeguards in accordance with Union and Member State law, including effective judicial remedy and due process",[24] so organisations will not be fined summarily. The Regulation also states that the fines are intended to be "effective, proportionate and dissuasive",[25] so you can assume that the intent is that they aren't needed: the threat of such fines should, ideally, ensure that all data controllers and data processors comply.

Infringements of some Articles carry the maximum administrative penalty (as noted, up to four percent of annual global turnover in the preceding financial year, or €20 million, whichever is greater). These articles primarily relate to the data processing principles, data subjects' rights and international transfers of personal data.

The higher penalties apply to the following Articles:

- 5 – Principles relating to processing of personal data
- 6 – Lawfulness of processing
- 7 – Conditions for consent
- 9 – Processing of special categories of personal data
- 12 – Transparent information, communication and modalities for the exercise of the rights of the data subject
- 13 – Information to be provided where personal data are collected from the data subject

---

[24] EU GDPR, Article 83 (8).

[25] EU GDPR, Article 83 (1).

- 14 – Information to be provided where personal data have not been obtained from the data subject
- 15 – Right of access by the data subject
- 16 – Right to rectification
- 17 – Right to erasure ('right to be forgotten')
- 18 – Right to restriction of processing
- 19 – Notification obligation regarding rectification or erasure of personal data or restriction of processing
- 20 – Right to data portability
- 21 – Right to object
- 22 – Automated individual decision-making, including profiling
- 44 – General principle for transfers
- 45 – Transfers on the basis of an adequacy decision
- 46 – Transfers subject to appropriate safeguards
- 47 – Binding corporate rules
- 48 – Transfers or disclosures not authorised by Union law
- 49 – Derogations for specific situations

There is also a lower rate of penalty for infringing other Articles of the Regulation, which is calculated at up to two percent of global annual turnover in the preceding financial year, or €10 million – again, whichever is greater. This applies to the following Articles:

- 8 – Conditions applicable to child's consent in relation to information society services
- 11 – Processing which does not require identification

- 25 – Data protection by design and by default
- 26 – Joint controllers
- 27 – Representatives of controllers or processors not established in the Union
- 28 – Processor
- 29 – Processing under the authority of the controller or processor
- 30 – Records of processing activities
- 31 – Cooperation with the supervisory authority
- 32 – Security of processing
- 33 – Notification of personal data breach to the supervisory authority
- 34 – Communication of a personal data breach to the data subject
- 35 – Data protection impact assessment
- 36 – Prior consultation
- 37 – Designation of the data protection officer
- 38 – Position of the data protection officer
- 39 – Tasks of the data protection officer
- 42 – Certification
- 43 – Certification bodies

Principles

Article 5 of the GDPR outlines the six principles that should be applied to any collection or processing of personal data.

1. Personal data must be processed lawfully, fairly and transparently.

2. Personal data can only be collected for specified, explicit and legitimate purposes.

3. Personal data must be adequate, relevant and limited to what is necessary for processing.

4. Personal data must be accurate and kept up to date.

5. Personal data shall be kept in a form that permits the data subject to be identified for no longer than is necessary for processing.

6. Personal data must be processed in a manner that ensures its security.

It's worth noting that the data controller is responsible for demonstrating this, and they must secure the same assurances from any external data processors with which they contract.

These six principles are at the heart of the Regulation. You should be clear on what each of them means, however, especially as some terms are considerably broader than you might otherwise expect (such as 'processing' – a full definition is provided in the previous chapter).

Fundamentally, if you can demonstrate that you're meeting these requirements, it is likely that you're in a good position to meet the GDPR's compliance requirements, although there are other aspects of the Regulation that you must address.

Applicability

The GDPR applies to organisations within the EU, and to any external organisations that are processing the personal data of EU residents. This potentially includes organisations everywhere in the world, regardless of how difficult it may be to enforce the Regulation. Because the Regulation asserts that both the data controller and the data processor are liable in the event of a data breach, this extensive reach is likely to keep European organisations from working with companies and states that fail to meet the Regulation's requirements. With the impressively threatening fines hovering overhead like a sword of Damocles, there are few organisations that will be willing to risk working with an organisation outside the EU that cannot prove its ability to protect the personal data it is given.

The information that the Regulation aims to protect is that of "natural persons, whatever their nationality or place of residence". Although some commentary has claimed the GDPR applies only to EU citizens, it in fact accounts for all residents of the European Union, including refugees, people on work and travel visas, those with residency, and so on. Furthermore, EU organisations bound by the Regulation must protect personal data about *anyone* from *anywhere* in the world.

Naturally, this presents difficulties in enforcing the GDPR on organisations based outside the EU, but it is important to remember that the Regulation does not distinguish between data subjects on the basis of nationality or location; most processors based outside the EU are, in any case, required to have a nominated representative within one of the EU Member States.

The personal data that the Regulation refers to is much broader than that which was protected under the DPD and the varying acts of legislation that supported it. The GDPR states that the personal data it is concerned with is:

> any information relating to an identified or identifiable natural person ('data subject'); an identifiable person is one who can be identified, directly or indirectly, in particular by reference to an identifier, such as a name, an identification number, location data, an online identifier or to one or more factors specific to the physical, physiological, genetic,

mental, economic, cultural or social identity of that natural person;[26]

This extended list of characteristics means that a great deal of anonymised data that could be processed under the DPD may no longer be suitable for distribution or sharing in public. At the very least, organisations that distribute anonymised data should carefully assess whether the data can be linked – directly or indirectly – to the actual subject. This list of characteristics is also not exhaustive, so any information that could be used to identify the data subject should be subject to the same protections.

Data subjects' rights

The GDPR considerably increases the rights of data subjects. Much has been made of this in the news – especially the 'right to be forgotten' – but the Regulation does attempt to balance those rights against the right to the free flow of information in order to support "the pursuit of economic activities". The specific rights set out in the GDPR are as follows:

1. Right of access
2. Right to rectification
3. Right to erasure ('right to be forgotten')
4. Right to restriction of processing
5. Right to data portability
6. Right to object
7. Rights in relation to automated decision-making, including profiling.

---

[26] EU GDPR, Article 4 (1).

These rights are supported by general requirements around transparency that require the organisation to provide key information to data subjects.

The rights granted to data subjects can generally be characterised as giving them more control over their data and giving them a better understanding of what is being done with it.

From the organisation's point of view, this means that you need to be clear about what data you are collecting and what you will be using it for. This is critical because many of the restrictions on processing in the Regulation have caveats that apply if the data subject has explicitly consented. While you might not think that your particular data processing invokes one of these caveats, the actual rules on what can be done without specific consent are surprisingly restrictive.

Should their rights be infringed, data subjects can seek judicial remedies against controllers and processors, and have the right to seek compensation from controllers or processors for damages arising from breaches of the GDPR. Data subjects also have the right under Article 77 to lodge a complaint with their relevant supervisory authority if they believe the processing of their personal data infringes the GDPR. More generally, controllers are directly "liable for the damage caused by processing which infringes" the GDPR. As previously noted, this ensures that the controller has a vested interest in ensuring the security of any personal data that they pass to a processor, whether the processor is inside or outside the European Union.

Transparency

The rights afforded under the GDPR are all subject to the principle of transparency, which requires that the data controller provide key information about the processing – where possible, this should be before the processing itself commences.

The specific information that you must provide is set out in Articles 13 and 14. In general terms, this should include key contact information, the purpose(s) of the processing, lawful basis for processing, any additional recipients of the personal data, any international transfers that may take place and the measures to secure the personal data, and information about the data subject's rights and how to exercise them.

Many organisations provide this information in a template format via privacy notices, with the specifics of the processing itself added as supplemental information. For instance, you might provide the data subject with some core information about the processing activity and also direct them to a privacy notice that includes contact information and details about their rights.

Right of access (and data subject access requests)

Data subjects have the right to access the personal data that you hold on them. This also means that you must provide information about the processing itself. Much of this is, again, likely to be covered by privacy notices.

Requests for access are called data subject access requests (DSARs) and have been a source of a great number of complaints to supervisory authorities since the GDPR came into effect. As such, it is critical that your organisation has a clear and reliable process for responding to DSARs. Data subjects may also use DSARs to exercise their other rights.

Many organisations give data subjects direct access to their personal data via a portal on their website(s) – the 'My Account' section on Amazon is a good example. There, the user can not only review the personal data, but they can also easily assert several of their other rights, such as rectification.

Right to rectification

Data subjects have the right to ensure that personal data held on them is accurate and up to date. This applies not only to information that is fundamentally incorrect (such as having misspelled their name) but also to information that may change over time (such as their address).

Where the personal data is also processed by other parties, the controller is responsible for passing corrections along to data processors and other relevant third parties.

Right to be forgotten

Data subjects have the right to have any data held about them erased under a number of circumstances, and this must also occur if they withdraw consent for all of the processing for which the data is held. This is functionally quite a broad right. Organisations will not have a particularly large range of options for refusing to erase personal data, so should have a process to erase all such data as and when necessary and ensure that, if personal data has been passed to other processors, they too are notified of the erasure request.

While this might seem quite straightforward, the data controller must also take "reasonable steps" to erase any of the data subject's personal data that might be public, such as in news articles or databases. As anyone who understands the Internet knows, this is barely possible – the variety of archive databases assure that – but it is quite likely that the data protection authority in your country will still want to see that a concerted effort has been made, and that all appropriate technical and procedural measures to erase the data have been employed.

Right to restriction of processing

Data subjects may have processing limited or prevented under specific circumstances. These circumstances are as follows:

1. If the data subject contests the accuracy of the personal data held.
2. If the processing activity is unlawful but the data subject is opposed to simply deleting the data.
3. The controller no longer needs the data but the data subject needs it to be retained for a legal purpose.
4. If the data subject has objected to the processing (see the right to object below).

When processing must be restricted, this means that the personal data may only be processed with the data subject's consent, for the data subject's legal purposes, or for reasons related to the public interest.

The data controller is responsible for ensuring that any restrictions are also passed on to data processors.

Right to data portability

Under Article 20 of the Regulation, data subjects can request a copy of any personal data held on them, and can also request that this information is transmitted to another data controller. The Regulation doesn't stipulate precisely how this information has to be presented or the format it has to be in, but it does require that it is in a "structured, commonly used and machine-readable format".

While this shouldn't present too much of a difficulty to most organisations, determining an appropriate format before you're asked to supply the information is a sensible step. Much like freedom of information requests, the key is to ensure that the process is inexpensive and efficient. Banks in the UK, for instance, offer data portability through the use of midata, which is used to provide customers registered for online banking with access to their transactional data from their current accounts, which they can then upload to third-party websites.

Some businesses already have appropriate contact with other organisations to facilitate the transfer of data – as noted above, banks in the UK – and these contacts could be leveraged to streamline this process.

Right to object

Under some conditions, the data subject has the right to object to processing. These conditions are quite restrictive. Data subjects may only object to processing if it is:

1. Necessary for a task carried out in the public interest or in the exercise of official authority; or
2. In pursuit of the controller's legitimate interests.

Of note is that the GDPR explicitly states that "Where personal data are processed for direct marketing purposes, the data subject shall have the right to object at any time to [that processing]".

If a data subject makes a valid objection to processing, then all such processing of their personal data must stop (see the right to restriction).

Rights in relation to automated decision-making, including profiling

These rights relate to decisions that can have legal effects for the data subject. The data subject has the right to have such decisions made by a person (or some other non-automated process). There are some fairly strong limits on this right, however. The data subject cannot exercise this right if:

1. The processing is necessary for entering into or performing a contract between the controller and the data subject;
2. The processing is authorised by a Union or Member State law; or
3. The processing is based on the data subject's consent.

Lawful processing

As noted earlier, controllers are accountable for ensuring that personal data is lawfully, fairly and transparently processed. The lawfulness of processing is expanded in Article 6, which sets out a range of conditions under which processing is lawful. This includes processing under consent of the data subject, as well as processing necessary for certain tasks, the majority of which require consideration of the data subject's interests.

It is worth noting that processing is permissible if it is "necessary for the purposes of the legitimate interests pursued by the controller or by a third party, except where such interests are overridden by the interests or fundamental rights and freedoms of the data subject which require protection of personal data, in particular where the data subject is a child".[27] While this caveat essentially makes lawful any reasonable processing in line with your organisation's interests or the interests of third parties – including wider benefits to society – you must ensure that it does not otherwise threaten the interests, rights or freedoms of the data subject, and is not in contravention of some other law or regulation (at the local, national or Union level). Needless to say, organisations need to be careful to ensure that, where legitimate interests are used as the basis for processing, an appropriate legitimate interest assessment has been carried out and is documented. The European Commission provides some guidance on assessing the validity of legitimate interests.[28]

In addition to these requirements, personal data can only be processed for limited purposes, to a minimal extent and accurately. This ties into the requirement for transparency: the data subject must be aware of the nature of the processing, which will inform the 'limited purposes' and 'minimal extent'.

Processing special categories of data (e.g. ethnicity, sexual orientation, health, etc.) is explicitly forbidden except in very specific circumstances.[29]

---

[27] EU GDPR, Article 6 (1) (f).

[28] *https://ec.europa.eu/info/law/law-topic/data-protection/reform/rules-business-and-organisations/legal-grounds-processing-data/grounds-processing/what-does-grounds-legitimate-interest-mean_en*.

[29] EU GDPR, Article 9.

Consent

When the GDPR was first brought into effect, there was a visible rush from organisations all over the world seeking consent to continue holding personal data. While this was perfectly sensible in many cases, in others, it was founded on a misunderstanding of the GDPR. While consent is an important concept in the Regulation, it is also valuable to understand where it is not necessary. As noted above, consent is only one of the lawful bases on which you can process personal data.

Because of the many conditions that consent demands, it is better in most cases to identify an alternative lawful basis if at all possible. Most of the time, the lawful basis will be determined by the processing activity itself – holding someone's data so that you can provide them with services, for instance, is likely to be lawful on the basis of contract.

Where consent is required, data controllers need to ensure that they secure clear and unambiguous consent from the data subject before processing personal data. Critically, the controller is not permitted to count "Silence, pre-ticked boxes or inactivity"[30] as consent. Furthermore, processing cannot proceed unless the data subject has consented to every processing activity – if you wish to carry out six different actions with the subject's data, for instance, you need to ensure that the subject has consented to all of them individually.

This is quite a change from the requirements of the DPD, which permitted implicit and 'opt-out' consent under some circumstances.

---

[30] EU GDPR, Recital 32.

The Regulation notes that consent can be provided electronically using a tick-box (although, as noted above, the data subject must manually tick the box themselves), which is in line with the way many organisations ensure appropriate consent for specific activities. However, because of the notorious unreliability of the user with regard to terms and conditions (and because, in the past, companies have found themselves in court over the use of fine print in such documents), the GDPR requires that the consent document be laid out in simple terms. In the words of the Regulation, "the request must be clear, concise and not unnecessarily disruptive to the use of the service for which it is provided".[31] This final point can be problematic, especially where you require consent for a variety of activities.

Documentation of consent is crucial, and this is one key area in which legal input from your professional advisers is essential.

Finally, consent can be withdrawn. Few organisations have a formal, efficient process in place for allowing data subjects to remove consent, however, and – much like securing consent in the first place – the Regulation requires the data controller to provide a method whereby it is "as easy to withdraw consent as to give it".[32] Web application developers need to design and implement robust solutions to allow data subjects to withdraw their consent in accordance with this requirement.

Children's consent

Children under a certain age are unable to consent to having their personal data processed in relation to "information society

---

[31] EU GDPR, Recital 32.

[32] EU GDPR, Article 7 (3).

services".[33] The specific age at which a child can consent for these purposes is set by the Member State, and can range from 13 to 16. Obtaining consent from the holder of parental responsibility is therefore a chief concern for organisations that offer information society services to children.

Article 8 provides further information on this, but it does not describe specifically how to resolve the problem, nor how supervisory authorities might determine that you have met the requirements of the Regulation.

For organisations offering information society services to children in different Member States, it is incredibly important that any consent requirements are properly addressed in accordance with the law of the Member States in which the children reside. While many GDPR requirements are standardised across the Union, the age of consent can vary. This means that an organisation collecting personal data from children in Belgium may seek consent from children when they are 13, while consent from children over the border in France can only be sought when they are 15.

It is worth noting that these conditions only apply to consent for information society services. Consent for other purposes can be legitimately provided by children, provided that it is not in contravention of other Union or Member State laws.

---

[33] This is defined in Directive (EU) 2015/1535, Article 1(1)(b) as "any service normally provided for remuneration, at a distance, by electronic means and at the individual request of a recipient of services". Note that this age limit has been reduced to 13 in the UK.

Retention of data

As noted earlier, data subjects have the right to be forgotten, at which point the data controller must erase all information held on them. In addition to this, however, personal data can also only be retained for limited periods, which should be clear to the data subject at the point at which they consent. This isn't a hard and fast rule, of course, as some personal data could be held effectively indefinitely (by public bodies for specific governmental purposes, for instance) and other processing, by its nature, may be ongoing.

Regardless of how long you intend to retain personal data, confidentiality and integrity must be secured – including against accidental loss, destruction or damage. This is particularly important and should be an extremely high priority for every organisation, not least because of the compulsory data breach reporting (which is explained later). While it's true that this was a general requirement in almost all previous data protection regimes, you need to be sure that your information security practices cover the whole range of personal data – which, it's worth remembering, is much broader – and that your suppliers and partners have also understood and implemented this.

The "one-stop shop"

The GDPR is intended to be a single scheme, applied consistently across the EU in order to maintain a common market and support the free flow of information.

Each state determines a number of supervisory authorities or data protection authorities, which are the local point of contact for all GDPR issues. This is the "one-stop shop" mechanism, which is intended to reduce the bureaucratic load involved in dealing with potentially complex pan-EU issues of data protection, anonymity and so on. Each state has also determined a lead supervisory authority or data protection authority, which has appointed a member to the EU Data Protection Board described above. Many countries have not bothered with multiple supervisory authorities, simply because data protection is already centralised and there is little value in expanding the bureaucracy, but some non-unitary states have chosen to operate these authorities on a regional basis, with a lead supervisory authority established at the national level.

The EU Data Protection Board created by the GDPR has several duties, including ensuring that any measures developed and adopted in member countries are consistent with the objectives of the GDPR. The Board is composed of members of each Member State's lead supervisory authority, which should ensure that laws remain relatively consistent and have a minimal impact on commerce.

Organisations processing personal data across a number of EU Member States will deal with the data protection authority in their primary jurisdiction. This will cover all cross-border intra-EU data processing.

Records of data processing activities

Article 30 requires most data controllers to retain a record of their data processing activities. This record needs to contain a specific set of information such that it is clear what data is being processed, where it is processed, how it is processed and why it is processed.

Equally, data processors are required under the same Article to keep a record of all processing carried out on behalf of a data controller. It should be remembered that the definition of 'processing' is so wide that even organisations that solely store, erase or destroy personal data are considered to be processing it.

These records need to be made available to the supervisory authority on request.

Data protection impact assessments

What the GDPR calls data protection impact assessments (DPIAs) are mandatory for technologies and processes that are likely to result in a high risk to the rights of data subjects. Much like other impact assessments, you need to ensure that you take advice from an appropriate authority.

Article 35(4) states that supervisory authorities in each EU Member State must publish a list of the kind of processing operations that are likely to be high risk and require a DPIA. The EDPB has approved a comprehensive set of guidelines regarding DPIAs here: *https://ec.europa.eu/newsroom/article29/item-detail.cfm?item_id=611236*.

Fundamentally, a DPIA assesses the risk of harm or other negative impacts on data subjects so that they can be mitigated. While the GDPR only requires DPIAs for processing activities that are likely to cause harm, this may not always be immediately obvious. As such, the controller should have some method by which it can quickly assess new or changing processing activities to determine whether a DPIA is necessary.

Organisations should ensure that a DPIA is part of their risk assessment process regarding personal data, and is in line with their data protection by design and by default strategies. As part of this, it is, of course, crucial that the results of a DPIA be acted upon. Simply conducting a DPIA does nothing to protect the rights and freedoms of data subjects – you must also take appropriate steps to minimise the risk of harm.

While DPIAs can be cumbersome, a single DPIA can address a set of similar processing operations with comparable risks. This means that data controllers that run large numbers of processes on data sets can get a great deal of this burden out of the way relatively quickly.

Once again, the data controller is responsible for ensuring that DPIAs are conducted. It's not a requirement that the data controller actually performs the DPIA themselves, however, and in many cases where processing has been contracted to a third party, it may be more sensible to have it conducted by the data processor.

Data protection by design and by default

DPIAs neatly dovetail into considering data protection in the design phase of an application or process.

The notion of building privacy or data protection measures into applications and processes is not new. Nor is it new to consider privacy or data protection in the initial design phase, often called 'privacy by design'. The Regulation, however, makes this mandatory in Article 25. You should note that this includes processes, not just applications – if any of your processes could result in a loss of data protection, and you have not addressed this "by design and by default", you are likely to be held liable in the event of a data breach.

It is important to remember that the Regulation does not specify how much security you should apply, nor the specific measures you have to use – it's just a requirement for you to "implement appropriate technical and organisational measures".[34] The critical element of this will be ensuring that you can prove to the supervisory authority that you did indeed take data protection into account from the beginning of your design.

The Article does provide a caveat in that you can take the current state of the art into account (among other things), and it's possible that the only truly effective measure hasn't been invented yet, but it's unlikely to convince the supervisory authority. Instead, you'll probably be told that you should have determined that the risks were too great and that you shouldn't have gone ahead. That is, after all, part of considering the state of the art, and a significant part of data protection *by default*.

---

[34] EU GDPR, Article 25 (1).

Controller/processor contracts

Where a controller contracts with a processor to process personal data, that processor must be able to provide "sufficient guarantees to implement appropriate technical and organisational measures"[35] that processing will comply with the GDPR and ensure data subjects' rights are protected. This requirement flows down the supply chain, so a processor cannot engage a second processor without the controller's explicit authorisation, which, of course, also means that the second processor has to supply the same guarantees.

This is simple good practice to start with, so it should not present any significant difficulty to organisations that have robust information security practices in place for supplier contracts.

Regardless of your organisation's state of information security, you should ensure that contractual arrangements are reviewed and updated. Ensure that responsibilities and liabilities between the controller and processor are stipulated. You need to document data responsibilities very clearly to ensure there is no confusion, and you may have to accept that the increased risk levels and requirements for data protection measures may impact service costs.

Certifications to international standards, such as ISO/IEC 27001, are recognised as effective ways to demonstrate that appropriate technical and organisational measures have been implemented.

---

[35] EU GDPR, Article 28 (1).

The data protection officer

Many organisations are required to appoint a data protection officer (DPO). There are three conditions under which you need one:

1. If the data is processed by a public authority or body, except for courts acting in their judicial capacity.
2. If the controller's or processor's core activities consist of processing operations that require regular and systematic monitoring of data subjects on a large scale.
3. If the controller's or processor's activities consist of processing large quantities of special categories of data and personal data relating to criminal convictions and offences.

These conditions cover a large number of organisations, and it isn't unusual to see companies appoint a DPO even if they're not required to – it's quite possible that an organisation's ordinary business will one day spike or adjust slightly, which will suddenly require a DPO and, in any case, the range of requirements imposed by the GDPR on any organisation makes the appointment of an appropriately qualified person to this role a sensible risk-containment step.

The DPO is appointed by the data controller and, where relevant, by the data processor, and a group of controllers and processors can share a single DPO as long as they are "easily accessible from each establishment". This means that organisations that may not have the resources to appoint a DPO for their own purposes can work with other such organisations to ensure they comply with the GDPR.

While the GDPR does permit a DPO to hold other responsibilities (because in many cases the role will not be full time), case law indicates that this is something the organisation needs to be very careful about. In 2020, the Belgian Data Protection Authority fined an organisation that had appointed a head of department to the DPO role, stating that this person had a conflict of interests as their primary role as head of department meant that they were involved in determining the means and purposes of processing personal data. This is explicitly forbidden under the GDPR. To best avoid this risk, the DPO should either clearly have no involvement in personal data processing, or be employed under a service contract, as approved by Article 37(6). A number of suppliers offer these services.

DPOs must be qualified for the role on the basis of expert knowledge of data protection law and practices, and being able to meet the requirements of Article 39 – "Tasks of the data protection officer". The role must report directly to top management, which should help ensure that data protection remains a key concern for the board and senior managers, and also help to ensure they remain well informed.

Given the requirements around information security and continuity, DPOs need to be more than legal experts – they need a mix of qualifications that enable them to deal effectively with the legal requirements, as well as the operational requirement to demonstrate appropriate organisational and administrative measures.

The DPO's duties generally revolve around ensuring that the data controller and data processor comply with all relevant data protection legislation, especially the GDPR. They should also offer advice, monitor DPIAs and operate as the immediate contact for the supervisory authority. The DPO's contact details must also be included in a number of reports and also be published by the data controller or data processor; website privacy policies would be a sensible location for this.

Accountability and the board

Given the magnitude of potential fines, the rights of data subjects to bring cases and claim compensation, and the prevalence and effectiveness of cyber crime, a GDPR breach should be on the board's risk register, and should remain high on board and top management agendas.

It is also important to remember that, in most instances, the data controller is accountable for failures of any data processor. That is not to say that the data processor gets off scot-free – they will also be held accountable – but it is critical that the board and top management ensure that any third-party data processors they engage are operating in accordance with the Regulation, regardless of the jurisdiction in which they operate.

In addition to a DPO, there are a number of other roles that need a level of familiarity with the requirements of the GDPR: most HR staff, as well as middle and senior management in virtually any function that deals with personal data processed, stored or transmitted by the organisation. Staff awareness training should support the more focused training given to managers.

Data breaches

In addition to being damaging for business – even if the authorities don't get involved – data breaches are strictly regulated under the GDPR. Of particular note are the notification requirements. The Regulation requires the controller to notify their supervisory authority of any data breach that is likely to pose a risk to the rights and freedoms of a data subject. If that risk is 'high', the controller must also notify the affected data subject(s). Data processors that discover a data breach are required to notify the controller "without undue delay".

There are, of course, some exemptions to the rules on notification, but it is an essential part of best practice to ensure that you have processes in place to make these notifications in the event of a data breach. At the very least, your procedure for responding to a breach should include consulting with your DPO (if you have one) to confirm whether notification is necessary.

Data breach reports must be made within 72 hours of the data controller becoming aware of the breach where there is a risk to the data subject. If that requirement is not met, the eventual report must be accompanied by an explanation for the delay. The notification must follow a specific format, which includes a requirement to describe the measures being taken to address the breach and mitigate its possible side effects. Where the breach may result in a high risk to the rights and freedoms of data subjects, they must be contacted "without undue delay". This contact will not be necessary if appropriate protective measures – essentially encryption – are in place to eliminate danger to data subjects. Supervisory authorities generally provide a template or form for notifying them of data breaches, and it is valuable to be familiar with these so that you know what information will be necessary ahead of time.

Incident response and breach reporting processes should cover all potential cyber breaches. Continual testing and maintenance of these processes are important to ensure that you can meet the 72-hour deadline – and to demonstrate that you have taken action to protect data subjects' rights.

Encryption

It is sensible to review arrangements around database and endpoint encryption. Organisations should already be encrypting mobile devices but, given the extent to which encryption could mitigate the impacts of a data breach, they should also consider extending encryption to cover all of the data collection, processing and storage processes.

When considering encryption standards, you would do well to follow best practice and seek out only FIPS 140-compliant solutions. FIPS 140 is the Federal Information Processing Standard established by the US and Canadian governments that sets out requirements for cryptography (it is not an encryption method in itself); in fact, in many cases it is a legal requirement for cryptography modules to be FIPS 140-compliant. With that in mind, ensuring that your solutions meet this standard will not only protect personal data in line with the Regulation's requirements, it may also allow you access to new markets or clients.

It is also worth considering that encryption should not just be applied to storage of personal data, but may also be valuable (or necessary) for establishing secure connections when personal data will be transmitted. Encryption specialists will no doubt be aware that Secure Sockets Layer (SSL) encryption is no longer considered secure, and that Transport Layer Security (TLS) 1.2 or higher is the minimum for these connections. Over time, vulnerabilities may be found in other cryptographic protocols, so it is essential to maintain awareness of the protocols and their status.

International transfers

The GDPR deals specifically with situations where a controller or processor intends to transfer personal data outside the EU – including transferring personal data to 'international organisations'. International organisations are those that are established in two or more countries, including subordinate bodies.

International transfers such as these are only legal if they comply with the conditions laid down in Chapter V of the GDPR, which are designed to ensure that the protections afforded to EU residents are not undermined by the transfer. These conditions require specific safeguards to be in place, and on the condition that data subject rights and effective legal remedies are available.

It is important to keep an eye on requirements around international transfers as they are often subject to legal challenges. In 2020, for instance, the now-famous 'Schrems II' case resulted in the EU–U.S. Privacy Shield programme being found invalid.[36] In its findings on the case, the Court of Justice

---

[36] *https://iapp.org/news/a/the-schrems-ii-decision-eu-us-data-transfers-in-question/*.

of the European Union also clarified how standard contractual clauses should be applied.

Organisations based outside the EU should pay special attention to rules for international transfers because they also apply to transfers undertaken once the data has left the EU. As Article 44 states: "the conditions laid down in this Chapter are complied with by the controller and processor, including for onward transfers of personal data". For instance, if personal data is transferred from France to the US under standard contractual clauses, a transfer from the original recipient to another organisation in the US (or to another third country) must also meet GDPR requirements for transfers. Transfers of personal data into the EU are not bound by such requirements, but there may be local laws that require some equivalent.

Adequacy

The EU Commission recognises some countries as providing adequate protection for personal data. Transfers into those countries do not require any further contractual safeguards. A list of these countries is published and maintained, including noting where recognition has been removed.[37] Data controllers and processors can transfer personal data to those countries without any further authorisation or safeguards beyond those normally required under the GDPR.

The GDPR states that codes of conduct and certifications to international standards are means by which controllers and processors may be able to identify organisations that provide appropriate safeguards. In fact, the Regulation encourages

---

[37] *https://ec.europa.eu/info/law/law-topic/data-protection/international-dimension-data-protection/adequacy-decisions_en*.

supervisory authorities to draw up codes of conduct and to encourage the use of data protection certifications.[38]

As the controller and processor are accountable for the personal data they process, any agreement to transfer that data to a third party, outside the arrangements identified in the GDPR, is illegal. This is particularly important when considering Cloud providers.

It should be noted that breaches of the Articles covering international transfers are subject to the highest administrative penalty.

At time of writing, the UK is transitioning out of the European Union. While the UK's data protection regime is clearly in line with the EU's, there is no guarantee that it will be granted an adequacy decision. Consequently, transfers from the EU into the UK may need to rely on one of the other mechanisms.

Binding corporate rules

Outside of transfers to authorised entities or countries, international transfers can only take place if the controller or processor has put in place legally binding and enforceable arrangements to protect the rights of EU data subjects. For a group of undertakings or group of enterprises engaged in a joint economic activity, binding corporate rules approved by the supervisory authority is one such means. Any organisation can develop its own binding corporate rules to secure personal data when transferring it to another country. The Regulation is very clear, however, as to what these rules must cover, so you need

---

[38] EU GDPR, Article 57 (1).

to consult Article 47 of the Regulation, and any rules you develop must be approved by the supervisory authority.

Binding corporate rules approved by the ICO in the UK will not be valid for organisations in the remaining EU from 1 January 2021. Organisations affected by this should identify a new supervisory authority within the EU and take steps to have their rules amended as necessary and approved.

Standard data protection clauses

The GDPR does allow the use of standard contractual clauses (sometimes referred to as model clauses) approved by the EU Commission to enable the transfer of personal data to third countries. An organisation can also develop its own contractual clauses, but these will require approval from the supervisory authority before personal data can be transferred.

As part of the Schrems II decision, the Court of Justice of the European Union found that standard contractual clauses are not an instant solution to international transfers. Organisations must assess such transfers on a case-by-case basis to ensure that the personal data will indeed be subject to appropriate safeguards. This will need to consider the legal obligations on the recipient organisation, among other matters – an organisation that is required to subject personal data to government surveillance, for instance, may not be able to receive personal data from an organisation bound by the GDPR.

Additional considerations

The GDPR cannot be viewed in isolation and any organisation adopting a sensible approach to compliance needs to be aware of other legislation that may affect it. Below are two such pieces of legislation that will need attention.

Changes to the 'Cookies Law'

The 'Cookies Law' – properly called the Directive on privacy and electronic communications, or the ePrivacy Directive – was controversial when it came into force in 2011 and has remained so. While some authorities have since relaxed their initial declarations on enforcing the requirements (generally moving away from threats of action to simply providing advice and occasionally contacting organisations that make absolutely no effort), there are still a host of websites decrying the Directive as ineffective, annoying and ridiculous.

The GDPR itself mentions cookies only once (in Recital 30), but does so to clarify that a cookie could be interpreted as an online identifier, which means that in some circumstances it falls under personal data and, therefore, the data subject must consent. This means that notifications for this type of cookie should follow the normal rules for consent, and forces the supervisory authorities to act when non-compliance is discovered. This will not please the people who campaigned against the original Cookies Law (and continue to do so).

The European Commission, meanwhile, has published, as a proposal text, the ePrivacy Regulation. There is no clear date as to when this new regulation will be published or applied, as it has been through a number of revisions, most recently in March 2020. What we do know is that, like the GDPR, it will apply to any website serving EU residents and the fines will mirror those set out by the GDPR, so the stakes are high.

The ePrivacy Regulation aims to strengthen the rules on the protection of electronic communications, particularly expanding the scope to cover new technologies such as Voice over Internet Protocol (VoIP), web-based messaging and the Internet of Things (IoT).

In relation to cookies, it appears the new regulation will require browser settings to disable cookies and set 'do not track' by default. This will ensure cookies can only be enabled with the consent of the data subject and that consent will be subject to the GDPR's stricter conditions of consent.

Cookies deemed not to be privacy intrusive, such as those that track the contents of shopping carts on e-commerce sites and those used for Google Analytics, will not require consent.

So, while it's possible that cookies will need to be more rigorously announced and consented to, it is equally possible that specific uses will be unaffected.

Directive on security of network and information systems (NIS Directive)

The NIS Directive aims to protect critical services against the increasing threat of cyber attack. With fines mirroring those of the GDPR, and the same incident reporting timescales and accountability requirements, it certainly needs to be taken seriously. The Directive has now been transposed into law in every EU Member State, so there is, figuratively speaking, nowhere to hide.

Where the GDPR seeks to protect personal data and the rights of the data subject, the NIS Directive establishes a "competent authority" for cyber security in each Member State. These authorities are responsible for ensuring that national infrastructure is secure from cyber security threats and that the common citizen can have a degree of faith in the technologies they use daily. On top of this, a more secure national infrastructure is envisaged as having a positive economic impact because the stability and reliability of services will make it simpler to compete in the single digital marketplace.

The NIS Directive applies to two types of organisations: operators of essential services (OES), which covers critical infrastructure such as health, transportation, energy, digital infrastructure and water; and digital service providers (DSPs), which includes search engines, online marketplaces and Cloud computing service providers.

Organisations that are required to comply with the NIS Directive face further complexity when it comes to reporting threats and incidents. Different OES have different competent authorities, and may have to report to these under the NIS Directive as well as to the ICO if the breach is also reportable under the GDPR's requirements.

It should be noted that the UK government has stated that the NIS Regulations will remain in force following the transition period.

CHAPTER 4: COMPLYING WITH THE REGULATION

There are clearly a number of key points to observe in your approach to complying with the GDPR. Plenty of them will be resolved fairly simply and quickly, if only at the prompting of a third party or a DPO. Some, however, will require a great deal of work or specific expertise. This section of the book will discuss those things that are critical to observe and offer advice for staying on the right side of the law.

Repercussions

It's been mentioned several times already, but it's worth reiterating that the GDPR can levy considerable fines. For certain breaches of the Regulation, you could be fined up to €20 million or four percent of global annual turnover, whichever is greater. Note that the four percent is on turnover, not profit, and applies to the organisation's global turnover, so for large organisations this could be considerably more than €20 million, and for a number of companies could be close to or exceed a billion euros.

It should also be noted that some organisations that are not involved in data processing can also face legal repercussions. Certification bodies involved in certification schemes in accordance with the Regulation, for instance, can face fines if they are found to be shirking their responsibilities. As such, it's possible for a single data breach to affect a large number of organisations – the data controller, any number of data processors involved in the data breach, and the certification body that approved the data processing.

Because these administrative penalties can be applied so broadly, it is very important to understand your own obligations and exposure. If you are concerned that you might not be in compliance with the law, you should consult a legal expert.

It is also important to remember that these penalties are in addition to any other fines or legal costs that you may incur following a data breach. Although fines from other regulators are unlikely to match the costs meted out under the GDPR, the compounding effects of other punitive measures could be significant. For instance, failure to meet the requirements of the Payment Card Industry Data Security Standard (PCI DSS) could result in losing the ability to take card payments, civil disputes in court could result in additional fines, and reputational damage could strip you of your customers, clients and suppliers.

Ensuring that your organisation supports compliance with the Regulation from the very top is critical to meeting your obligations – it is difficult to implement all of the necessary measures without it. As such, anyone responsible for implementing and maintaining compliance will need to start by making this clear to their organisation's top management and ensuring that it is understood. Reiterating the severity of the punitive measures, potential compensation claims and reputational damage – especially when set against the relatively low cost of compliance – is likely to get their attention.

Understanding your data: where it is and how it is used

The GDPR deals with existing personal data as well as with how that data is to be processed, transmitted and stored in future. For most organisations, the first step towards compliance is a data audit to identify the personal data the organisation holds, who it has been shared with and where it is now held. This will help determine what must be done with that data in order to comply with the GDPR.

The data audit process includes reviewing existing processes for gathering personal data, ensuring there are clearly identified business and legal grounds for that collection, and ensuring that all related processes comply with the Regulation. Depending on the nature of your business, this could prove to be quite a broad exercise, showing points of egress and ingress where personal data goes out to a processor and the processed result returns (assuming that the results of processing include personal data). You also need to be quite clear about the information assets that actually constitute personal data – photographs, for instance, can be used to identify an individual and so will almost always be regarded as personal data.

You should also consider where the data resides physically. If you use a Cloud solution, for instance, you will need to know where the Cloud supplier is based and, if it's not in the EU, whether it is able to provide sufficient assurances that it meets the Regulation's requirements (including, crucially, legal protections for data subjects and the presence of effective legal remedies). Equally, you should be sure to note any physical records of personal data that you might keep, including HR records, historical records (assuming the subjects are still living) and so on.

Data audits should be repeated periodically to make sure that they are thorough and that any new or changed processing is taken into account.

It is sensible to carry out a DPIA in relation to information that you have already collected, in addition to any DPIAs necessary for future processing. This should highlight any weaknesses in your current operations.

Documentation

The Regulation can require quite a bit of documentation. In addition to the explicit and implicit requirements for specific records (such as proof of consent from data subjects), you should also ensure that you have documented how you comply with the GDPR so that you have some evidence to support your claims if the supervisory authority has any cause to investigate. If you suffer a data breach, for instance, being able to demonstrate that you have consistently applied best practice, that you have an audit trail showing that you notified them and any affected data subjects within the required timeframes, and that you have taken all the appropriate steps to mitigate the impacts of the data breach, will minimise the chance that you will be hit with a crippling fine.

There are different documentation requirements for data controllers and data processors, but the onus for the documentation being correct is generally on the controller because they're likely to suffer the consequences regardless of who is at fault. If you are a controller with a number of outsourced processing functions, it's worth gaining assurances that these functions are appropriately documented by the data processors.

The following documentation is especially important, although it varies between data controllers and processors:

- Statements of the information you collect and process, and the purpose for processing.[39]
- Records of consent from data subjects or their holder of parental responsibility.[40]
- Records of processing activities under your responsibility.[41]
- Documented processes for protecting personal data – an information security policy, cryptography policy and procedures, etc.

---

[39] Full requirements in EU GDPR, Article 13.

[40] Full requirements in EU GDPR, Articles 7 and 8.

[41] Full requirements in EU GDPR, Article 30.

**Appropriate technical and organisational measures;
ISO/IEC 27001 and ISO/IEC 27701**

Article 24 says that data controllers must implement "appropriate technical and organisational measures to ensure and to be able to demonstrate that the processing is performed in accordance with the Regulation". This Article makes it clear that these measures must include implementing appropriate data protection policies. Similarly, Article 32 also requires "appropriate technical and organisational measures" to ensure the security of personal data. This clearly shows that the Regulation requires a double approach: measures that protect the rights and freedoms of data subjects, and measures that protect the security of the personal data itself.

Critically, both articles state that controllers can use adherence to approved codes of conduct or management system certifications "as an element by which to demonstrate compliance" with their obligations and the Regulation's requirements.[42] While it's likely that supervisory authorities will develop their own schemes and trust seals in the future, and that they'll recognise certain standards as meeting the GDPR's core requirements, achieving certification to a widely recognised information security standard will not only help to meet the requirements, it will also provide a good basis for attaining any necessary certifications or requirements that may arise in the future.

An ISO/IEC 27001 information security management system (ISMS) should be the starting point for organisations seeking to ensure they can demonstrate "appropriate technical and organisational measures" with respect to their GDPR obligations related to the security of personal data. This can be bolstered by

---

[42] EU GDPR, Article 24 (3).

ISO 27701, which acts as an extension to ISO 27001 and supports data protection activities related to data subjects' rights and freedoms.

The ISO 27001 risk-based approach to selecting information security controls is reflected in the GDPR requirement that controllers and processors should, on the basis of and proportionate to identified risk, implement appropriate technical and organisational controls to:

- Ensure the ongoing confidentiality, integrity, availability and resilience of processing systems and services;
- Ensure the security of the personal data; and
- Ensure the ability to restore availability following an incident.

They should also have a process for regularly testing, assessing and reviewing the effectiveness of the selected measures. As ISO/IEC 27001 is the only independent, internationally recognised data security standard that also has a widely accepted certification scheme, it seems logical that ISO 27001 – with in-built and appropriate business continuity arrangements, and supported by ISO 27701 – should be fundamental to organisational GDPR compliance strategies.

The fact that ISO 27001 is also the default management system for protecting organisations against cyber crime doubles its benefit. Cyber crime is not directly addressed in the Regulation, but it is an increasingly common cause of data breaches, and is regularly associated with the largest and most damaging breaches. ISO 27001 can also support compliance with the NIS Directive.

Implementing an ISO 27001 and ISO 27701 system for managing information security and data protection involves building a holistic framework of processes, people and technologies. It should address the organisation's internal and external contexts – such as the requirements of the GDPR – and the needs of interested parties, which would naturally include data subjects and supervisory authorities. Once established, the management system should systematically reduce information security risks on an ongoing and evolving basis through a process of self-examination and remediation. Crucially, the measures that you implement to secure information are taken on the basis of a thorough risk assessment that identifies threats and vulnerabilities affecting the organisation's information assets (which will certainly include any personal data or processing of personal data).

While such a management system can take some time to develop and mature, it is an excellent first step in demonstrating that you take data protection seriously, and the costs of implementation can often be offset by the efficiency improvements and improved market position.

Any appropriate trust marks should be integrated into the management system as they become available.

Standards, schemes and trust seals

Compliance with ISO/IEC 27001 helps organisations demonstrate that they have endeavoured to comply with the GDPR's requirements.

The Regulation mentions approved certifications and schemes, which may be developed locally (by supervisory authorities, for instance) or across the EU (by the Commission or EU Data Protection Board, for instance) to prove compliance with a set of practices that meet the requirements of the GDPR. Such schemes to provide GDPR-specific certification have yet to emerge, and it will be some time before there is clarity on this front.

It's also possible that some form of trust seal may be developed, much like the SOC 3 audit (but hopefully more affordable). In the meantime, organisations should adapt an existing ISO 27001 management system, or start working toward ISO 27001 with a strong GDPR emphasis via ISO 27701, perhaps with ISO/IEC 27018 (code of practice for protecting personal data in the

Cloud) and BS 10012 (specification for a personal information management system) included in the scope. Some certification bodies already conduct audits that include ISO/IEC 27018 in the management system scope.

Securing supplier relationships

The data audit described earlier helps you identify which of your supplier relationships need to account for the Regulation due to the movement of personal data between each party.

The most obvious upshot of this is reviewing your various contracts with third parties. You should ensure that your service-level agreements, and procurement and outsourcing processes, are reviewed in line with the GDPR's requirements. This is especially important if you are the data controller in the relationship, as you are equally liable for any breaches that occur as a result of a supplier's failure to preserve data protection. This should also include restrictions on the use of processors further down the supply chain in order to ensure the security of personal data at every point in the processing.

You also need to check your suppliers of Cloud services, remote servers and so on. While these are remote services, they're often integrated into the organisation's business practices as if they are managed locally, so it can be easy to forget about them. As noted earlier, you should also ensure that these service providers are either within the EU, or that you are able to preserve the relationship through safeguarding measures such as binding corporate rules or contract clauses. If you cannot secure these assurances, or there is difficulty having the service provider approved under the Regulation, you'll need to secure a more local or trustworthy supplier.

It is important to remember that many such arrangements will need to be revisited in light of the Schrems II decision. This is not limited to those that were lawful by way of the Privacy Shield – the decision may also affect personal data transfers under standard contractual clauses. One of the key outcomes of the case was that all such transfers must take the context of the recipient into account.

In addition to ensuring that the organisations you work with are in compliance with the Regulation, you also need to ensure that any data transfers are secure. This is a more practical consideration (use of encryption, etc.), but it should also be agreed with the supplier and included in contracts and service-level agreements.

CHAPTER 5: INDEX OF THE REGULATION

Chapter I – General provisions

1. Subject-matter and objectives
2. Material scope
3. Territorial scope
4. Definitions

Chapter II – Principles

5. Principles relating to processing of personal data
6. Lawfulness of processing
7. Conditions for consent
8. Conditions applicable to child's consent in relation to information society services
9. Processing of special categories of personal data
10. Processing of personal data relating to criminal convictions and offences
11. Processing which does not require identification

Chapter III – Rights of the data subject

Section 1 – Transparency and modalities

12. Transparent information, communication and modalities for the exercise of the rights of the data subject

Section 2 – Information and access to personal data

13. Information to be provided where personal data are collected from the data subject
14. Information to be provided where personal data have not been obtained from the data subject
15. Right of access by the data subject

Chapter VI – Independent supervisory authorities

Section 1 – Independent status

Section 2 – Competence, tasks and powers

Chapter VII – Cooperation and consistency

Section 1 - Cooperation

Section 2 – Consistency

Section 3 – European Data Protection Board

Chapter X – Delegated acts and implementing acts

Chapter XI – Final provisions

CHAPTER 6: EU GDPR RESOURCES

GRC International Group has a number of resources to simplify GDPR compliance. These range from books like the one you're reading (but generally more detailed), documentation toolkits and training courses, through to data flow audits and consultancy.

Certified GDPR Foundation Training Course

This comprehensive training course offers a solid introduction to the GDPR and provides a practical understanding of the implications and legal requirements of the Regulation, culminating in an official certification from the International Board of IT Governance Qualifications (IBITGQ).

www.itgovernance.co.uk/shop/product/certified-eu-general-data-protection-regulation-foundation-gdpr-training-course

Certified GDPR Practitioner Training Course

This course covers the GDPR in depth, including implementation requirements, the necessary policies and processes, and important elements of effective data security management.

www.itgovernance.co.uk/shop/product/certified-eu-general-data-protection-regulation-practitioner-gdpr-training-course

IT Governance Training Centre

IT Governance is committed to upholding the highest standards in health and hygiene, with safety a priority. That's why our new, purpose-built, training centre in Ely, Cambridgeshire has been verified under the NQA COVID SECURE Guideline Verification Scheme, designed with comfort, convenience, health and safety in mind.

This state-of-the-art, world-class venue seamlessly brings physical and virtual audiences into one live, collaborative experience, allowing you the flexibility of attending either in person, or online without losing the benefits of classroom learning.

For more information, visit: *www.itgovernance.co.uk/ely-training-centre*.

EU GDPR Documentation Toolkit

A full set of policies and procedures to enable your organisation to comply with the GDPR, these templates are fully customisable and significantly reduce the burden of developing the necessary documents to achieve legal compliance.

www.itgovernance.co.uk/shop/product/eu-general-data-protection-regulation-gdpr-documentation-toolkit

EU General Data Protection Regulation (GDPR) – An implementation and compliance guide, Fourth edition

This comprehensive manual provides detailed insights into the GDPR and offers practical advice on setting up and managing a privacy programme.

www.itgovernancepublishing.co.uk/product/eu-general-data-protection-regulation-gdpr-an-implementation-and-compliance-guide-fourth-edition

GDPR Gap Analysis

This service provides an assessment of your organisation's current level of compliance with the GDPR and identifies key priorities to address.

www.itgovernance.co.uk/shop/product/gdpr-gap-analysis

DPO as a Service

Outsourcing DPO tasks and duties to a managed service provider gives you access to expert advice and guidance to help you address the compliance demands of the GDPR.

www.itgovernance.co.uk/shop/product/dpo-as-a-service-gdpr.

GRCI Law

GRCI Law is a legal, risk and compliance consultancy firm, advising clients in the fields of data protection, data privacy, cyber and information security law.

For more information about the services that GRCI Law offers, visit: *www.grcilaw.com/topic/gdpr*.

DQM GRC™

As a wholly owned subsidiary of GRC International Group plc (LSE:GRC), DQM GRC are part of a leading global supplier that boasts of an extensive one-stop-shop for governance, risk and compliance products and services.

For more information about the services that DQM GRC offer, visit: *www.dqmgrc.com*.

FURTHER READING

IT Governance Publishing (ITGP) is the world's leading publisher for IT governance and compliance. Our industry-leading pocket guides, books, training resources and toolkits are written by real-world practitioners and thought leaders, and are used globally by audiences of all levels, from students to C-suite executives.

Our high-quality publications cover all IT governance, risk and compliance frameworks and are available in a range of formats. This ensures our customers can access the information they need in the way they need it.

For more information on ITGP and to view our full list of publications, please visit
www.itgovernancepublishing.co.uk.

To receive regular updates from ITGP, including information on new publications in your area(s) of interest, sign up for our newsletter at
www.itgovernancepublishing.co.uk/topic/newsletter.

Branded publishing

Through our branded publishing service, you can customise ITGP publications with your company's branding.

Find out more at:
www.itgovernancepublishing.co.uk/topic/branded-publishing-services.

Related services

ITGP is part of GRC International Group, which offers a comprehensive range of complementary products and services to help organisations meet their objectives.

For a full range of GDPR resources, please visit *www.itgovernance.co.uk/shop/category/data-protection-eu-gdpr*.

Training services

The IT Governance training programme is built on our extensive practical experience designing and implementing management systems based on ISO standards, best practice and regulations.

Our courses help attendees develop practical skills and comply with contractual and regulatory requirements. They also support career development via recognised qualifications.

Learn more about our GDPR training courses and view the full course catalogue at *www.itgovernance.co.uk/training*.

Professional services and consultancy

We are a leading global consultancy of IT governance, risk management and compliance solutions. We advise businesses around the world on their most critical issues and present cost-saving and risk-reducing solutions based on international best practice and frameworks.

We offer a wide range of delivery methods to suit all budgets, timescales and preferred project approaches.

Find out how our consultancy services can help your organisation at *www.itgovernance.co.uk/consulting*.

Industry news

Want to stay up to date with the latest developments and resources in the IT governance and compliance market? Subscribe to our Weekly Round-up newsletter and we will send you mobile-friendly emails with fresh news and features about your preferred areas of interest, as well as unmissable offers and free resources: *www.itgovernance.co.uk/weekly-round-up*.

EU for product safety is Stephen Evans, The Mill Enterprise Hub, Stagreenan, Drogheda, Co. Louth, A92 CD3D, Ireland. (servicecentre@itgovernance.eu)

www.ingramcontent.com/pod-product-compliance
Lightning Source LLC
Chambersburg PA
CBHW071552080326
40690CB00056B/1807